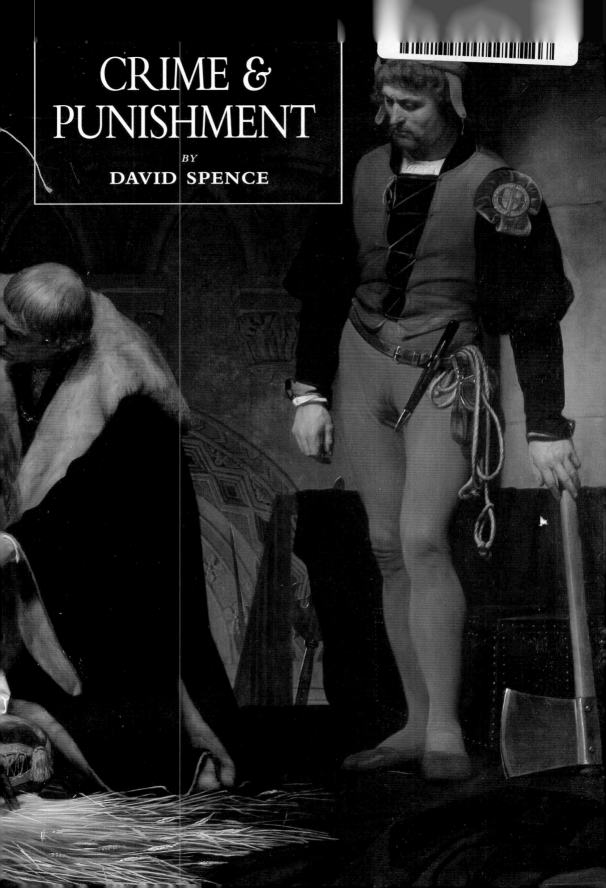

CRIME & PUNISHMENT

BY
DAVID SPENCE

WHAT IS A CRIME?

*E*very society in every age has lived by a set of rules which determined what was permissible and what was forbidden. The rules, which gradually became the written laws, helped everyone live together harmoniously and were generally accepted. Those who did not abide by the rules offended against the conventions of society. Such people are called criminals although in earlier times they were known as felons.

HUMILIATION

Public humiliation, such as forcing a drunkard to 'wear' a barrel, acted as a deterrent to others.

NOT SO FUNNY MONEY

Any forging or defacing of money was treated very seriously. This imitation note was called a 'Bank restriction' note by its creator, George Cruikshank. He made it to draw attention to what he thought was unfair punishment after he had passed two women hanging from the gallows outside Newgate. Their crime was to have passed forged one pound notes. Cruikshank's satirical imitation note was so popular he sold thousands at a shilling each. The governors of the Bank of England 'were exceeding wroth' but since that time no other person has been hanged for the crime.

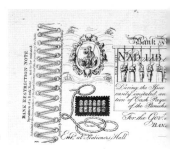

PUNISHMENT OF THE ENVIOUS

Religious law and secular law were very closely associated in earlier times, thus people believed offenders could incur punishment in this life and in the next. In this medieval picture those guilty of envy are continually moved back and forth between tanks of boiling and freezing water by pitchfork wielding devils.

IRON MASK

This grotesque iron mask is probably a scold's bridle. The mask contained a metal plate which was forced into the scold's mouth to prevent speech.

A WOMAN'S LOT

Women were expected to obey men (they were once 'chattels', or the property of men) and meet standards of behaviour set by men. One of the 18th-century punishments for women who led a disorderly life was shaving the head.

JUSTICE, PURITY AND HOPE

Women seldom enjoyed the same rights as men in the eyes of the law, which was of course written by men. Emmeline Pankhurst (pictured above) led the suffragettes who fought for women's rights, most notably the right to vote. Their official colours were purple for justice, white for purity and green for hope.

THE SCOLD

Public humiliation was often used both to punish wrongdoers and to set an example to others. Here a 'scold' (a gossip) wears her bridle. Perhaps this is linked to a time when idle talk could be dangerous; in the 17th-century it was possible to condemn a complete innocent to death by verbal evidence alone.

LAWMAKERS

arly English codes of law stressed compensation rather than retribution. During the reign of Ethelbert in the 7th-century the fine for murder was 100 shillings; 12 shillings for severing an ear. The influence of the church became profound. Fines were paid to the clergy and to the King. Under King Canute mutilation became common; an adulteress forfeited nose and ears. Slaves, men without property and women had no esteem in religious or secular law. Eventually the concept of sin and retribution came together until execution replaced compensation in response to law breaking.

MAGNA CARTA

This document of 1215 drawn up by the rebellious barons and signed by King John laid down important principles of law. It stipulated that 'no freeman shall be arrested, imprisoned, disposed or in any way injured banished or hurt... save by the lawful judgement of his peers or the law of the land'.

LAW OF EMPIRE

At the height of British power British lawmakers sat in judgement all over the world. After 1698 the East India Company gained the right in Calcutta to administer justice, including the power to hang Indians.

THE KING'S COURT

The King's bench, situated in Westminster Hall, was the highest court in the land. The King formerly sat in person at this court. This 15th-century representation depicts shackled prisoners as they wait their turn in the dock.

PUT TO THE TEST

In the middle ages innocence or guilt used to be judged by ordeal. One such ordeal was for the accused to place his bandaged hand in boiling water; after three days the bandages were removed and if the hand was uninjured God had declared innocence. Any scald mark was the anger of heaven and the accused was punished accordingly for the crime.

COMMON LAW

This manuscript illustration is from a record of the customary law of the Saxons, dating from the early 13th-century. It illustrates the divorce procedure of the time. A priest separates the spouses; the woman holds the child and also shears, representing the wife's property which she retains.

LAW OF GOD

The Bible recounts how God called Moses on Mount Sinai and gave him the ten commandments on two stone tablets. For many years crimes against religious laws were punished in the same manner as crimes against property or people. Heretics were always put to death.

BELIEF & PUNISHMENT

Belief was the foundation upon which order was built throughout much of our history. When in 1533 Henry VIII broke with the Church of Rome and declared himself Supreme Head of the Church of England the resulting reformation brought harsh punishments to those who stood in its way. Everyone had to swear an oath to the King as Supreme Head of the Church. Refusal to swear was high treason. Failure to do so resulted in punishment in this world – usually a terrible death by burning or being hanged, drawn and quartered – and eternal damnation in the next.

TITUS OATES

The division between Protestant and Catholic belief was manipulated by Oates who spread word of a Catholic uprising in London in the 1670s, causing widespread hysteria. Oates was eventually punished severely.

SURVEY OF THE MONASTERIES

In 1535 royal officials toured the monasteries at Henry VIII's behest, submitting a report to the King. It described the monks and nuns as wicked and superstitious. The report's outcome was determined in advance. It gave the King an excuse to dissolve the monasteries, executing monks who resisted.

ROAST IN HELL

People were fearful of what would happen to them after their death and this would influence the way they behaved. A heretic (a person who disagreed with the religious teachings of the time) would be burned. One of the most famous executions was the burning in 1556 of Archbishop Cranmer.

LONDON BRIDGE

Severed heads atop London Bridge used to be a common sight. One of the better known to end up there belonged to Bishop John Fisher who was executed for treason in 1535. Fisher's crime was to deny that the King was the Supreme Head of the Church. His head was parboiled and displayed on a pole. The crowds passing over the bridge commented that it grew 'fresher and more comely every day'.

GUY FAWKES'S LANTERN

This is the lantern (or lanthorn as it was then called) with which Fawkes was found as he crouched in the cellar beneath the Houses of Parliament and with which he planned to light the slow fuse connected to 36 barrels of gunpowder.

REMEMBER REMEMBER

Guido Fawkes (known today as Guy), an explosives expert with the Spanish army, was recruited by Robert Catesby to assassinate the protestant King and leadership in 1605 by blowing up Parliament. The plot was uncovered, Fawkes arrested and tortured until he revealed his true identity. Fawkes was hanged, drawn and quartered along with his fellow conspirators.

SUPERSTITION

Fear of witchcraft was widespread for many centuries. In the 16th-century laws were passed which laid down the death penalty for witchcraft, enchantment or sorcery. Because the crime was unprovable by nature, suspicion was sufficient grounds for accusation and proof could be as slight as an unnatural mark on the body. According to one account witches could be identified by their habit 'of throwing back their hair and intertwining their fingers'.

DAEMONOLO-
GIE, IN FORME
of a Dialogue,
Divided into three Bookes.

DAEMONOLOGY

James I was particularly concerned about witchcraft, so much so that he recorded his views in a book published in 1603 entitled Daemonology.

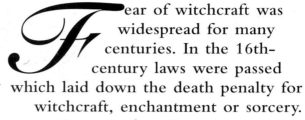

JAMES I

King James was permitted to use torture under Scottish law, something forbidden under English law. Once when subjected to a stormy sea crossing James accused one Dr Fain of brewing the storm. Fain did not confess under traditional means of torture so James suggested a new device: 'his nailes upon all his fingers were riven... and under everie nayle was thrust in two needels'. Fain was eventually burned alive.

Convicted witches were hanged or burnt depending on
the circumstances of the crime. Most witches,
but not all, were women. As a rule the
witch was mercifully strangled before
being burnt, but the Earl of Mar's
account of one incident tells how a
women broke free of the slow fire
and the spectators (burnings always
drew huge crowds) threw the
poor woman back into
the flames.

BIER PROOF

One very strange superstition is illustrated here.
The accused is naked and tied by the waist with
a length of rope. He is then made to approach
and touch the 'mortal wound' on the body of
the deceased as it lies in its coffin. If the wound
subsequently starts to bleed the
accused is guilty of murder!
In this example from the
Lucerne Chronicles (1513)
the accused was in fact convicted
of the murder of his wife.

INITIATION

This medieval
illustration
shows
initiation
rites for
witches.
It reflects
contemporary
fears of the
unknown at a time when protection
against disease and illness relied as
much on pagan ritual and charms
as on medicine.

THE BLOODY TOWER

Raleigh's confinement in the Tower for treason lasted many years during which time he drafted a five-volume history of the world. He eventually died a nobleman's death – losing his head to the axe.

'In truth there is no sadder spot on the earth' wrote Thomas Macaulay of the Tower of London. The Tower has witnessed the Kings and Queens of England pass through its gates since its construction by William the Conqueror in the 11th-century.

CHOPPING BLOCK

This is the block upon which the Scottish rebel Lord Lovat placed his head in 1747. Lovat told the executioner 'Cheer up thy heart, man; I am not afraid; why should you?'. The executioner severed Lovat's head with a single blow.

THE WHITE TOWER

A series of walls, gateways, bastions and towers were gradually built around the central 'White Tower', so called because it was built on a hill known as 'White Hill'. The exterior wall, built with pulverized Roman red tiles and bricks, looked as if 'built with mortars tempered with the blood of beasts'.

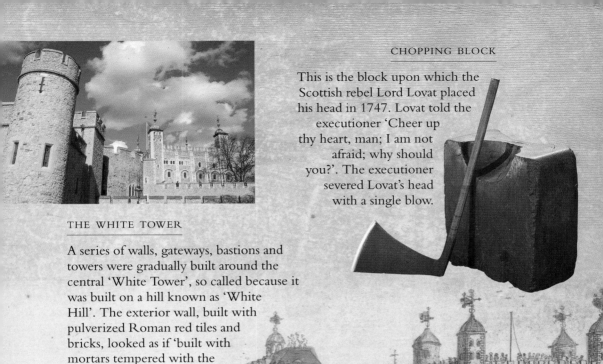

TOWER HILL

Public executions took place on the hill just outside the Tower: only very important prisoners had the privilege of privacy and were executed within the walls. This print shows the public execution of the Jacobite rebel Lords Balmerino and Kilmarnock. There were also casualties amongst the thousands that had assembled to watch the execution. One of the spectator stands overlooking the scaffold collapsed crushing several people to death.

VICTIMS OF THE THRONE

*M*any have died for King and Country, not least members of the royal family and those close to it. Rivalries for the throne have in the past caused terrible suffering as varying factions fought for control.

In Tudor times if a courtier was arrested as a traitor the other courtiers wrote to the King denouncing the traitor immediately because if convicted his estate would be divided amongst the critics. The family of the accused would also write denouncing their own kinsman, hoping to keep the estate in the family.

LADY JANE GREY

Jane Grey acceded to the throne at the age of fifteen thanks to the political manipulations of her father in law, the Duke of Northumberland. Her reign of nine days was ended by supporters of her cousin, Mary, who ordered her execution.

DEATH WARRANT

This is the death warrant of Charles I, signed by 59 republicans. Charles Stuart was charged with treason because he 'levied war against the Parliament and kingdom of England'.

Lord Darnley married Mary Queen of Scots in 1565. Darnley fell out of favour with Mary who spent more time with her Italian Secretary, David Riccio. Darnley killed Riccio in a fit of jealousy. Mary was to be avenged for this act.

This contemporary drawing shows the ruins of Darnley's house which Mary had blown up in revenge for Darnley's actions.

Darnley's infant son, James, calls for vengeance from his cradle. James would become King of England.

Darnley's body lies beneath a tree. He was strangled before he could escape his murderers.

THOMAS BECKET

Becket, Archbishop of Canterbury, had defied King Henry II's demands to control the power of the church. Henry's rash words to the 'idle cowards who stand by while this miserable priest insults me to my face' caused four of his courtiers to put Becket to death within his cathedral. One of the assassins dealt Becket such a blow that his sword broke in two. Just four years later, in 1174, Becket was canonised 'Saint Thomas'.

A DOOMED MAN

The day before his execution Charles spoke to his son, Henry, 'Do not let them make thee king, for they will cut of thy brothers heads when they can catch them, and cut off thy head too, at the last'.

TERRIBLE PUNISHMENTS

For most of our history punishments have been both painful and public in order to act as a deterrent to others. Physical retribution against the offender was considered more important than incarceration. Physical punishments and public humiliations were social events and carried out in the most accessible parts of towns, often on market days when the greater part of the population were present. Justice had to be seen to be done.

TURKISH BUTCHER

If a Turkish Butcher was found guilty of selling bad or short weight meat he was tied to a post with a piece of stinking meat fixed under his nose.

THE HALIFAX GIBBET

The guillotine was used in England probably before it was introduced into France and was known as the Halifax Gibbet. The device was employed in the town of Halifax between 1541 and 1650. Felonies to the value of 'thirteen pence halfpenny or more' were punishable by execution.

THE WHIP

Whipping was a common punishment which was also favoured by the Navy to maintain discipline.

The notoriously vicious Judge Jeffreys once passed sentence thus, 'I charge you to pay particular attention to this lady. Scourge (whip) her soundly, man; scourge her till the blood runs down'.

TURKISH BAKER

The Criminal Recorder was published in 1804. It was *an account of the various punishments inflicted on those who have transgressed the laws of their country.* In this illustration a Turkish baker is nailed to his door by one ear as a punishment for selling short weight.

BRANDING

Branding was used for centuries to mark an offender permanently, usually on the cheek or hand, sometimes in the shape of a letter such as V which represented vagabond. In 1630 a preacher named Leighton was found guilty by the Star Chamber of criticising the King. He was branded on the face with SS (Sower of Sedition) as well as having his nose slit, his ears cut off and soundly flogged, before being imprisoned for life.

THE THUMBSCREW

This instrument probably derived from a medieval hand crushing device known as the pilliwinks. The thumbscrew was commonly employed to restrain prisoners in the manner of handcuffs.

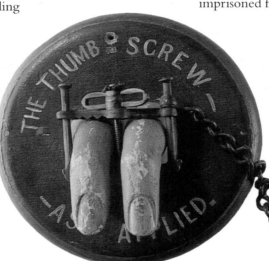

THE PILLORY

One of the most common punishments for petty offences was the pillory, which stood in the main square of towns up and down the country. The offender was locked by hands and head into the device and made to stand, sometimes for days, while crowds jeered and pelted the offender with rotten vegetables or worse!

LAUGHING STOCK

Public humiliation was increased by the custom of forcing the offenders, who were tethered to posts or locked in stocks, to wear ridiculous masks and mocking signs around their necks.

...TERRIBLE PUNISHMENTS

*T*orture was forbidden in England by the Common Law of the land. The Magna Carta expressed fundamental rights including freedom from torture. However in Tudor and Stuart times prisoners were tortured by Royal prerogative which overruled Common Law. This was achieved by setting up tribunals which were not bound by Common Law. The most famous of these were the Star Chamber and the Ecclesiastical Court of High Commission.

THE BOOT

'...an iron boot was placed about the lower leg and wedges driven into the boot so crushing the flesh and bone'

GUILLOTINE BLADE

This much-used blade formed part of a portable guillotine and was captured from the French revolutionary forces in 1794. The blade, mounted on a sliding block, weighs 63lbs (28.5 kilos).

DRAWN ASUNDER

An account of the trial of the assassin of Henry IV of France tells how the accused is tied to four horses to tear him apart.

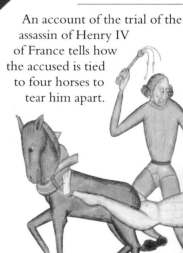

STRANGULATION

The *Criminal Recorder* of 1804 tells us that strangulation was the accepted method of execution in Turkey in the 18th-century.

THE RACK

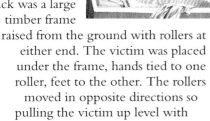

Frequently used in England, the rack was a large timber frame raised from the ground with rollers at either end. The victim was placed under the frame, hands tied to one roller, feet to the other. The rollers moved in opposite directions so pulling the victim up level with the frame, stretching every ligament and eventually dislocating every joint in the body.

STONING

This medieval manuscript illustration shows an ancient method of punishment, that of stoning. One of the 'crimes' that was punishable by this method in some parts of the world was adultery.

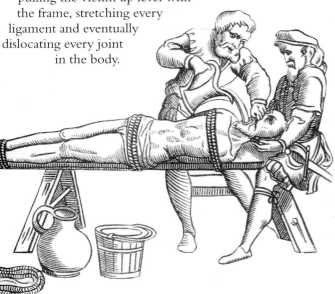

WATER TORTURE

A gauze bag, placed in the throat of the victim, was slowly filled with water poured by the torturers. As the bag filled it slowly pushed its way down into the stomach.

DUCKING

The ducking stool was often found by the village pond and used for minor misdemeanours. Ordeal by water was also used in witch trials to 'discover' witches. The accused was cross-bound (right toe to left thumb, left toe to right thumb) and flung into a pond. Floating indicated witchcraft, drowning proved innocence.

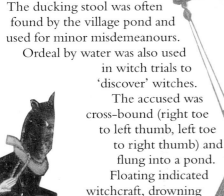

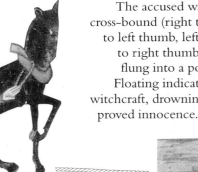

BEHEADING

Beheading was normally reserved for those of high rank. In England a block and axe was the common method but this was different from France and Germany where the victim kneeled, as pictured, and the head was taken off with a swing of the sword. This was the method requested by Anne Boleyn and used for her beheading.

ARISTOCRAT OF THIEVES

Today highwaymen are thought of as gallant knights of the road but the truth was very different. Generally highwaymen were ruthless killers. In one account the son of a surgeon, William Cady, shot a passenger who had swallowed her wedding ring in order to protect it. Cady was not to be frustrated by her actions. He proceeded to cut her open to retrieve the ring.

DICK TURPIN

Turpin was a notoriously violent housebreaker. His gang, the 'Essex Gang' pillaged and raped, terrorising London and the surrounding area.

MOLL CUTPURSE

The Jacobean Highway-woman Mary Frith went by the name of Moll Cutpurse. A big strong woman, fond of smoking and drinking, she continued her successful career of highway robbery for many years dying of disease at seventy-five years of age.

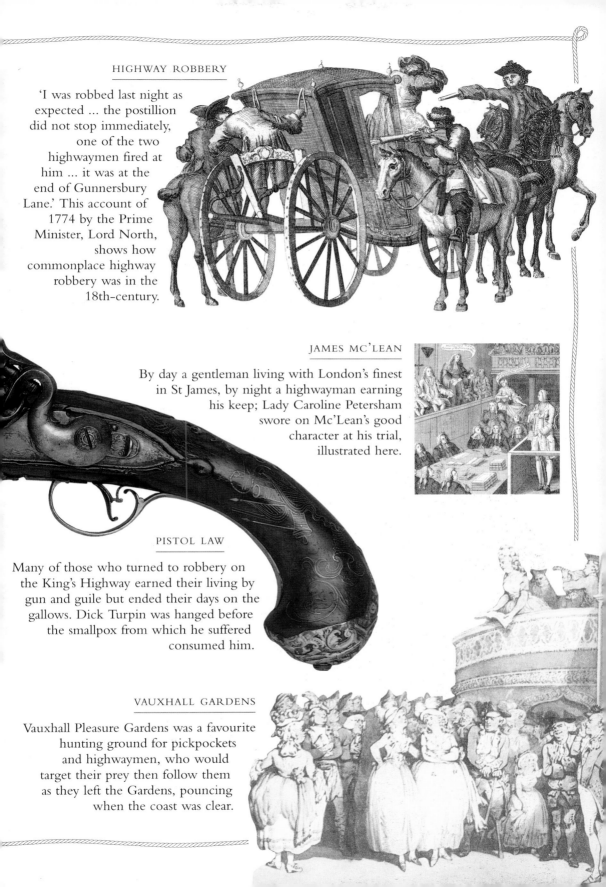

HIGHWAY ROBBERY

'I was robbed last night as expected ... the postillion did not stop immediately, one of the two highwaymen fired at him ... it was at the end of Gunnersbury Lane.' This account of 1774 by the Prime Minister, Lord North, shows how commonplace highway robbery was in the 18th-century.

JAMES MC'LEAN

By day a gentleman living with London's finest in St James, by night a highwayman earning his keep; Lady Caroline Petersham swore on Mc'Lean's good character at his trial, illustrated here.

PISTOL LAW

Many of those who turned to robbery on the King's Highway earned their living by gun and guile but ended their days on the gallows. Dick Turpin was hanged before the smallpox from which he suffered consumed him.

VAUXHALL GARDENS

Vauxhall Pleasure Gardens was a favourite hunting ground for pickpockets and highwaymen, who would target their prey then follow them as they left the Gardens, pouncing when the coast was clear.

THE ROAD TO TRIPLE TREE

*I*n the 18th-century there were literally hundreds of offences which incurred the death penalty. It was typical for the Old Bailey to be in session from 6.30am to 9pm, hearing 20 cases a day. Most were tried for stealing property, like John Williams, hanged in 1747 for stealing a pair of breeches. Many public hangings occurred at the Tyburn gallows (the site in London now known as Marble Arch). The three uprights of the gallows led to one of its many names - the triple tree.

SILK HANGINGS

Thousands were employed in the silk weaving trade. The silk weavers attempted to control prices in order to gain a fair wage and weavers who charged less than the 'book price' had their looms sabotaged. Parliament supported the cheaper prices and made it a hanging offence to sabotage looms.

HANGING JUDGE

Judge Jeffreys was a brutal man who ordered the execution of over 300 men, women and children at the Winchester Assizes in 1685, following the failed rebellion of the Duke of Monmouth. Jeffreys had little regard for the jury; if they failed to convict he would order them to find the accused guilty.

END OF THE ROAD

The condemned were drawn on carts to the place of execution, sometimes already wearing the shroud in which they would be buried. Thousands of spectators would gather to watch the hanging.

BLACK PEW

Monday was hanging day in Newgate Prison; the preceding Sunday saw the prisoners who were condemned to die seated around a coffin which was placed on a table within the 'dock' of Newgate chapel. The prisoners seated in the 'black pew' and the sightseers who had purchased places in the chapel gallery had to listen to the 'condemned sermon'.

THIEF–TAKER GENERAL

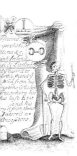

Underworld figure Jonathan Wild 'arrested' thieves for money. This mock ticket to an execution invites felons to 'triple tree'.

DYING CONFESSIONS

The prison cleric, known as the 'Ordinary', talked to the condemned in the cells in the last days before execution. He summarized the conversations which told the sorry story of the condemned and published them, for personal profit, on execution day.

DANCING THE PADDINGTON FRISK

'...**Y**ou must be led to the place of execution and when you come there you must be hanged by the neck till you are dead and your body be dissected and anatomised'; so read the sentence that condemned many to the gallows, or in slang terms to *go west* (literally, from Newgate to Marble Arch) or *dance the Paddington Frisk*. There was in fact a more dramatic punishment whereby victims were hanged, drawn (taken down alive), had their intestines removed and burnt before their eyes, beheaded and cut into four quarters.

DEATH SWEAT

It was believed that the touch of the hanged man's hand possessed healing properties. Women would allow the dead man's hand to brush their affliction or that of their children.

SPORT

The death of others was considered perfectly good entertainment and in fact hanging days at Tyburn fair were treated as holidays, drawing huge crowds.

DISSECTION

It was considered a further punishment on the condemned to order that their body be anatomised. The dissected body would be publicly displayed in the Surgeon's Hall to add to the humiliation.

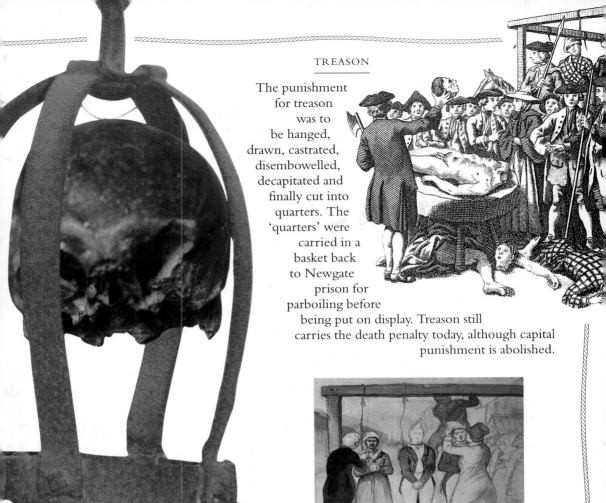

TREASON

The punishment for treason was to be hanged, drawn, castrated, disembowelled, decapitated and finally cut into quarters. The 'quarters' were carried in a basket back to Newgate prison for parboiling before being put on display. Treason still carries the death penalty today, although capital punishment is abolished.

A TERRIBLE END

Death by hanging meant death by strangulation until the refinement of the 'drop' which broke the victim's neck. Relatives or friends sometimes hung onto the victim's writhing body, the additional weight speeding death. Eventually the trapdoor was introduced, breaking the victim's neck quickly. Before the refinement of the 'drop' the heavier victims risked decapitation as their bodies suddenly plunged downwards.

THE GIBBET

Gibbeting of corpses was commonplace. The victim's corpse would be placed in a set of chains known as a gibbet cage, and hung at a cross-roads or similar public place. This skull belonged to John Breads, executed and gibbeted for the murder of Allen Grebell in the town of Rye in 1742.

AVOIDING THE DROP

Prison births were common as there was no segregation between the sexes.

There were a number of ways to avoid the hangman's noose. 'Benefit of Clergy' was applicable in some cases. This meant that if you could recite the 51st Psalm (the neck verse) you demonstrated your literacy, and therefore worth and were saved. Lesser punishments such as flogging, imprisonment or transportation awaited those who escaped the gallows. Their fate was uncertain and often led to death by a different path.

BEATING HEMP

Houses of Correction were established to give work to vagrants and the unemployed. Bridewell was such a place and this illustration shows inmates beating hemp.

THE PRISON HULKS

Many prisoners were confined in hulks of ships moored in ports. Conditions here were worse than in normal prisons. Hulks housed many prisoners-of-war as well as being a staging post for those destined for transportation to the colonies.

THE TREADMILL

The prisoner's survival rate was poor. Gaol fever (typhus) killed thousands, starvation killed yet more. Many prisons were privately owned and the owners turned a good profit by selling gin and by releasing prisoners who could afford to pay their way out.

BRIDEWELL

Situated in Bridge Street, Blackfriars, Bridewell Prison was but one of many in London. This scene shows the Pass-Room, where 'miserable females are confined for 7 days before being sent off to their respective parishes'.

PEINE FORTE ET DURE

If prisoners refused to plead they were pressed to death. The one advantage for the prisoner in dying in this manner was that by law his estate might pass to his heirs, whereas the estate of a hanged man was forfeit. Pressing meant the victim was placed in a low dark room, laid on his back and tied in a spread-eagle position while weights were continually added to his chest, eventually crushing him to death.

HARD LABOUR

Prison labour was often put to constructive use on building projects and other public works. Here prisoners help construct a new dock at Woolwich.

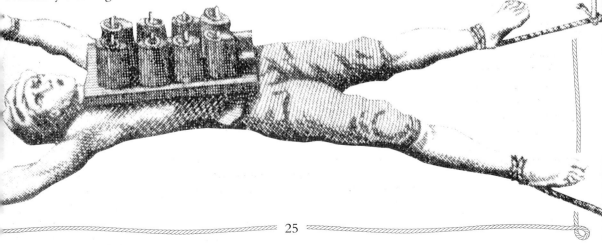

HOUSE OF DESPAIR

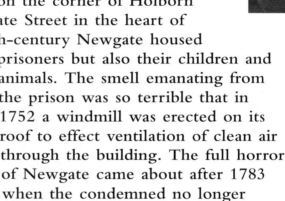

Of all the prisons, Newgate was the most notorious. The building was situated on the corner of Holborn and Newgate Street in the heart of London. In the 18th-century Newgate housed prisoners but also their children and animals. The smell emanating from the prison was so terrible that in 1752 a windmill was erected on its roof to effect ventilation of clean air through the building. The full horror of Newgate came about after 1783 when the condemned no longer made the journey to Tyburn but were hanged outside the walls of the prison. To escape the terrible life inside the gaol prisoners brewed their own gin, calling it 'kill-grief'.

PRISON LIFE

In 1818 a member of parliament visiting Newgate complained of the gross scenes of depravity. Prison officers were bribed to allow whores to visit on a daily basis.

THE HUMAN ZOO

The behaviour of inmates in hospitals for lunatics were regarded as entertainment. People paid to visit and stare just as people today visit animals in a zoo.

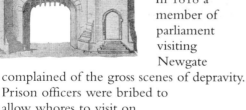

DEBTORS PRISON

Fleet Prison housed debtors. It was sometimes in the financial interests of the inmates to marry and marriages within Fleet Prison, performed without clergymen, were recognised by law.

JACK SHEPPARD

The infamous housebreaker Jack Sheppard is probably Newgate's best known prisoner. In 1724 Sheppard was imprisoned for robbing a house. In three hours he had escaped. He was captured and put in the securest part of Newgate; again he escaped despite being locked in irons and chains. Sheppard's escapes passed into popular culture, inspiring plays and songs.

DARTMOOR PRISON

Dartmoor was chosen as a near perfect site on which to build a prison. It had a plentiful supply of fresh water, peat for burning and granite blocks for building. It housed many prisoners-of war during the Napoleonic wars.

MADNESS

Sufferers of mental illness were locked up in institutions such as the Hospital of Bethlem (Bedlam) or St Luke's Hospital for Lunatics which was a grand building designed by George Dance in 1782.

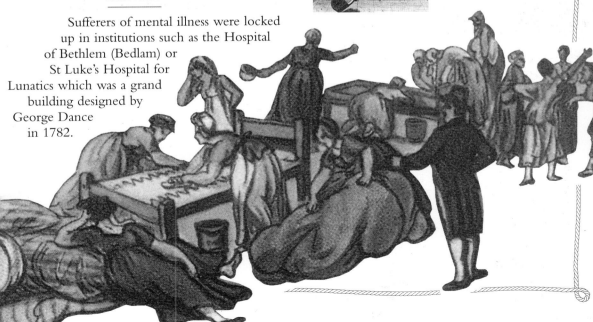

CONVICT SHIPS

*I*n 1718 the Transportation Act initiated the process of systematically transporting those pardoned for hanging offences. Attempting to return to England before serving the full sentence was itself a hanging offence. At first ships carried felons across the Atlantic to North American towns such as Annapolis but from 1776 the War of American Independence made the authorities seek alternative destinations. In 1788 the first small fleet of ships carrying about 775 prisoners arrived in Botany Bay, Australia.

KANGAROO ISLAND

Depicted here in this painting by Westall, the remote Kangaroo Island became a retreat for 'white pirates'. These were chiefly escaped convicts who lived beyond the law and abducted Aborigines into slavery.

UNDER GUARD

The transport ships had to be converted below decks to accommodate their human cargo. Reinforced bulkheads and hatch bars were fitted. Royal Navy ships accompanied the transport and supply ships. This model of a Royal Navy frigate illustrates the type and size of the ships that sailed the 15 thousand miles across the world.

BOTANY BAY

The first fleet of 11 ships arrived at Botany Bay but found it an unsuitable place to land. Exploring further along the coast the fleet finally came to a suitable natural harbour on the 26 January 1788. This is known today as Sydney Harbour.

GONE FOREVER

This illustration reveals a poignant moment; the sister weeps on her brother's shoulder as he waits, leg in irons, to be led to the transport ship. Conditions on board were harsh and many did not survive the journey.

HUMAN TRADE

In the 1720s the Government paid contractors to transport convicts to America, paying up to £5 per person. On reaching their destination the convicts were sold at a profit.

RACE RELATIONS

Sir George Arthur, Lieutenant-Governor of Van Dieman's Land, had notice boards erected (such as the above example of 1828) promising equal justice regardless of the colour of skin. This graphic illustration was particularly addressed to the Aborigines.

PROTECTION
& DETECTION

An early type of policing was introduced in the middle ages, known as 'watch and ward'. From this term derived 'watchmen'; men chosen from all householders in the community to protect citizens at night. In the 1760s the Bow Street police office opened. It was here that crimes were recorded and from here that horse patrols guarded the roads. This was the beginning of an organised and accountable police force.

THE NIGHT WATCH

Watch houses were established under the control of constables. The watchmen assembled at the watch house to collect their long staff and lantern; those apprehended for crimes during the night were held at the house until they could be delivered to the magistrate.

CRIMINAL SIGNATURE

The discovery that every person's fingerprint consists of a unique pattern of whorls and ridges and that no two patterns are the same was a huge leap forward in crime detection. From this time police were able to match a print left at the crime scene with a suspect's finger; a match could mean only one thing – the suspect was there.

Index

PEELERS

In the 1820s Robert Peel was responsible for the *Bill for Improving the Police*. The policemen, or 'peelers', wore top hats and blue tail-coats with identifying numbers on the collar.

ROBBERS

Stealing was not just a way of life but a means of survival. The poor were very poor and often desperate, a good wage being hard to come by.

POLICE FOR HIRE

Until organised law enforcement came about in the late 18th-century many different types of voluntary and private 'policemen' existed. The rich could hire men for protection or to arrest those guilty of theft or debt. In this painting from the *Rakes Progress* series the ominous prospect of prison looms in the shape of Newgate in the background while the Rake struggles with the constables.

CRIMINAL MIND

Some people believed that criminals were born criminals. Caesare Lombroso, a Professor at the University of Turin in the 19th-century, argued that criminals were physiologically different from honest people; criminals retain primitive instincts destitute of morality. His theory somehow never accounted for the fact that children of virtuous parents can turn to crime!

CRIMINAL BODY

In the 19th-century police attended classes at which they were taught to identify typical physical characteristics of the criminal class. For a time people really believed you could tell a criminal by his face.

A GLOSSARY OF INTERESTING TERMS

Benefit of Clergy - originally a church privilege which decreed that clergy guilty of committing felonies should not be hanged. This form of reprieve was later extended to felons who could read the 51st Psalm (the neck verse).

Whipped at the cart-arse - the offender was whipped while tied to a slow moving cart as it passed through the streets.

Hue and Cry - an alarm sounded by the justice of the peace which signalled that every member of the parish should turn out to hunt down the criminal.

Crack Lay - housebreaking.

Black Art - lock picking.

The Charm - lock picking tool.

Blood Money Act (1692) - an act which decreed that an award of 40 pounds was payable for the apprehension, prosecution and conviction of a highway-robber.

Buttered Bun - prostitute. Also known as Moll, Froe, Bunter, Smut, Trumpery, Crack.

Nanny House - brothel.

Cunning Man - parish detective. He determined guilt or innocence in Tudor times by ritual, such as writing suspect's names on pieces of paper which were subsequently wrapped in clay and submerged in water. The first name to come to the surface was the guilty one.

Bung - a purse.

Cutpurse - a thief who literally cut (or nipped) the money purse of the belt, rather than the pickpocket (foist) who dipped his hand in the bung.

A Doxy - a female tramp.

Vagabond - the name for outcasts who roamed the streets begging or earning their living by dubious means. A succession of laws attempted to control the vagabond. An Act of 1572 punished a vagabond thus 'to be grievously whipped and burned through the grissel of the right ear with a hot iron an inch wide'. The second offence was hanging unless someone agreed to employ him; the third offence always hanging.

His Majesty's Seven Years Passenger - a criminal transported to the colonies.

Rhino - money. Also known as quidds and spanks. Particular denominations had special names such as 'yellow boy' (1 guinea) and 'pig' (6 pence).

ACKNOWLEDGEMENTS

We would like to thank: Mark Leeds, Tim Feeley, Graham Rich, Tracey Pennington and Peter Done for their assistance. We are particularly indebted to Peter Linebaugh's work *The London Hanged*, Liza Verity for the use of her personal library and the library of the National Maritime Museum.
Printed in Italy - Copyright © 1995 ticktock Publishing Ltd.
First published in Great Britain by ticktock Publishing Ltd., Great Britain. All rights reserved.
No part of this publication may be reproduced, stored in a retrieval system, or transmitted in any form or by any means, electronic, mechanical, photocopying, recording or otherwise, without prior written permission of the copyright owner.

Acknowledgements: Picture Credits t=top, b=bottom, c=centre, l=left, r=right
Abbreviations NMM=National Maritime Museum MK=Mittelalterliches Kriminalmuseum
Ashmolean Museum, Oxford; OFCr/7r. Bodleian Library, Oxford; 3tr (Roll 208G.frame 1), 5tr (215.3.10), 5br (215.3.1), 6/7ct/32 (218.9.15), 8tl/9br (163A2.19), 16/17cb (Series B), OFCbr/17tr (165E.30), OBCbr/17cr (2153.16), 22tr (215.3.17). British Museum; 6/7c. Cathedral Gifts Ltd; 12/13c. E.T. Archive; 3bl. Graves Art Gallery; 20cb. Guildhall Art Gallery, Corporation of London/Bridgeman Art Library; IFC/1. The Honorable Society of the Inner Temple/E.T. Archive; 5tl. House of Lords Record Office, London; 12b. John Falconer; 4b. Mary Evans Picture Library; OFCc/30cl, 30/31c. MK; 3ct, 8/9cb, 15br, 17cb. Musee des Beaux-Arts, Rouen/Lauros-Giraudon/Bridgeman Art Library; 23cr. Museum of London; 10/11. NMM; OFCtr, OBCbl, 8bl, 10tr, 13br, 14cb, OBCcr/14bl, 16c, OBCcl/18/19c, 19t, 20l, 22l, 24cb, 25cb, 27c, 28tr, 28/29tc, 28bl. Mr Palmer, Rye Town Hall; 22/23c. Public Record Office; 6br (E344/22), 13tr (MPF366-1). Royal Armouries; OFCtl/2tr, 11tr, 15c. By courtesy of the Trustees of the Sir John Soane's Museum, London; 26/27ct, 31tr. Tasmanian Museum & Art Gallery; 29tr.

Every effort has been made to trace the copyright holders and we apologise in advance for any unintentional omissions. We would be pleased to insert the appropriate acknowledgement in any subsequent edition of this publication.

A CIP Catalogue for this book is available from the British Library. ISBN 1 86007 010 8